WHAT KIND OF DOG IS THAT?

LoLo Smith

Illustrations by Gloria Marconi

©2020 LoLo Smith
Background illustrations and book design
© 2020 Gloria Marconi Illustration & Design

All Rights Reserved.
Printed in the United States through Kindle.

Published by Do The Write Thing of DC
Email: dothewritething1@gmail.com
Website: dothewritethingdc.org

Follow the author on social media:
facebook.com/lolo.smith.169405
Instagram @lolosmith2016

Other Books by LoLo Smith

Max & Bo: Two Dogs On The Go
Ten Acts of Kindness
My Doll & Me: Superheroes Fighting Bullying with Kindness
Say No To Bullying - Say Yes To Kindness
Community Workers & COVID-19 (A Children's Book About Coronavirus)
The Little Town of Share-A-Lot
I Know My Community Workers
El Cuento del Medallon de Oro/The Tale of the Gold Medallion
Sista CindyElla Mae, The African-American Cinderella

All of these books are available for free download at
authorsden.com/author/lolosmith
Please write a review at amazon.com if you enjoy the books.

Follow the author on social media at
facebook.com/lolo.smith.169405
Instagram @lolosmith2016

BASSET HOUND

The **Basset Hound** is a short-legged breed of dog in the hound family. Its short legs are due to a form of dwarfism. The Basset comes from France and is a hunting dog. Basset Hounds are often called hush puppies.

Like the Bloodhound, it has a sad look, but it is friendly, outgoing, playful and likes being around children.

It lives about 10 years.

BORDER COLLIE

The **Border Collie** is from Scotland and England. It is used to herd sheep so it is also called a Sheepdog. It is the most intelligent or smartest of all dogs. It is very energetic, acrobatic and athletic so it likes to chase moving cars, trucks and bicycles.

This is a high energy dog that likes lots of exercise. If it stays in the house all day, it will chew holes in walls and furniture.

It lives for about 12 or 15 years.

BULLDOG

The **Bulldog** is from England. The English brought bulldogs to America. Bulldogs are friendly and make good pets for children.

The bulldog is used as a mascot for many universities.

Bulldogs live for about 6 years.

CHIHUAHUA

The **Chihuahua** is the smallest breed of dog. It is named after the state of Chihuahua in Mexico.

This dog is easily frightened and will attack small children. The Chihuahua gets cold easily and burrows in pillows, clothes hampers and blankets. It is like a cat and climbs to the highest point on a couch then curls into a ball.

Chihuahuas live from 12 to 20 years.

GERMAN SHEPHERD

The **German Shepherd** is a large working dog from Germany. It looks like a wolf. This dog was first used for herding sheep but because of its strength, intelligence, trainability and obedience, it is used for many types of work. It is used as a guide dog for the blind, for search-and-rescue, by the police and military and even for acting!

The German Shepherd is the second most popular dog in the United States. There was a famous German Shepherd named Rin-Tin-Tin who was on a television show and has a star on the Hollywood Walk of Fame.

German Shepherds live for about 10 years.

LABRADOR RETRIEVER

This is a popular dog around the world that is trained to help people who are blind. It also acts as a therapy dog. It helps detect drugs for the police.
It is also a hunting dog.

The Labrador Retriever is kind, pleasant and outgoing so it is very good with children.

The Labrador Retriever lives for about 12 years.

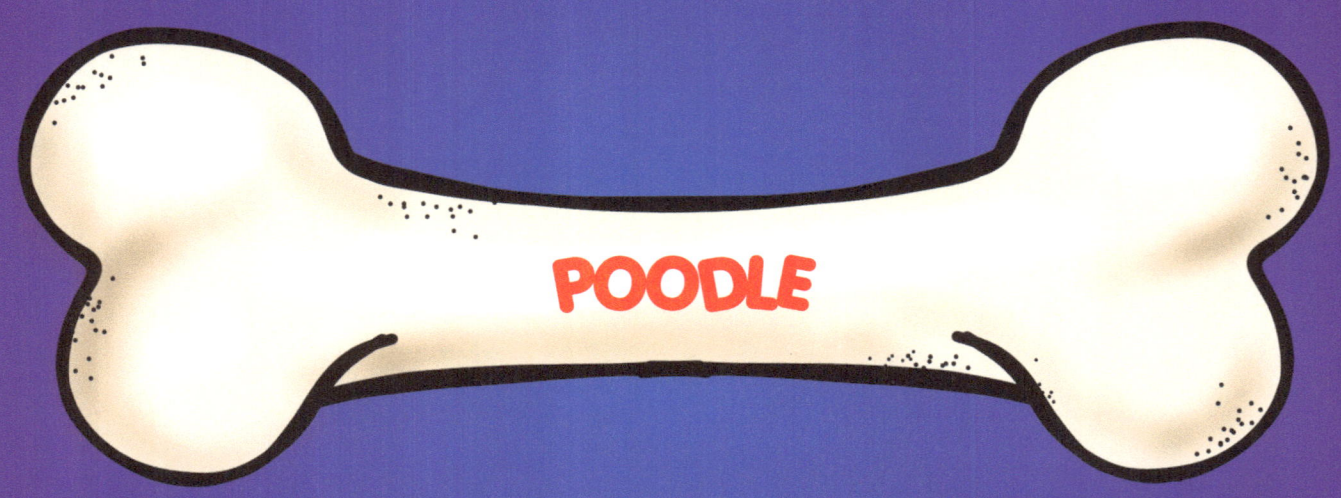

POODLE

The Poodle is a dog breed that comes in three types:
Standard Poodle
Miniature Poodle
Toy Poodle

The **Poodle** is the second most intelligent dog breed. It is skillful at dog sports, swimming and activities such as circus performances.
It also makes a good assistance dog.

Standard Poodles live 11 or 12 years.
Miniature and Toy Poodles live 14 or 15 years.

SCHNAUZER

This dog breed comes from Germany. The name "schnauzer" comes from the German word for "snout" or "moustache" because the dog has a bearded snout. There are three types of Schnauzers: Miniature, Standard and Giant. This dog was used as a rat-catcher and guard dog. The police and military use the Giant Schnauzer.

The Schnauzer is a smart dog that likes daily exercise.

WESTIE

The Westie is the short name for the West Highland White terrier, a breed of dog from Scotland.
This dog is smart, quick to learn and can be good with children.
The Westie is very popular in the United States and is used in the TV commercial for Cesar dog food. This type of dog has also been in movies, on television shows and in books.

Westies live from 8 to 16 years.

JUST FOR FUN

1. Point to the **Poodle**.
2. Point to the **German Shepherd**.
3. Point to the **Bulldog**.
4. Point to the **Chihuahua**.

JUST FOR FUN

1. Point to the picture of the **Westie**.
2. Point to the picture of the **Basset Hound**.
3. Point to the picture of the **Border Collie**.
4. Point to the picture of the **Labrador Retriever**.

FREE DOWNLOAD OF PAGES OF DOGS FOR CHILDREN TO COLOR

To obtain a free download of 11 pages of pictures of dogs for your child to color,
Email dothewritething1@gmail.com

Follow the author on social media:
facebook.com/lolo.smith.169405
Instagram @LoLosmith2016

ABOUT LOLO SMITH

LoLo Smith is an educator, writer and creator of Living Storybook, a literacy program for young children. She has written 9 books for children on topics such as kindness, bullying, careers, the holidays and COVID-19. Her books feature community workers, superheroes, American Girl® dolls, anime characters, community workers and dogs! Her books for children come with free downloadable companion gifts. See all of her books at amazon.com/author/lolosmith and follow her on social media facebook.com/lolo.smith.169405 or Instagram @lolosmith2016.

ABOUT GLORIA MARCONI

Gloria Marconi is an illustrator and graphic designer working in the Washington, DC area for over 40 years. A multi-faceted artist, Ms. Marconi specializes in print and works in a variety of media ranging from traditional to quilting to computer-generated illustration. Over the years, her clients have run the gamut from corporations to government to non-profits as well as editorial illustrations for books, magazines and advertising. Here is a portrait of her granddog, Diesel, a black German Shepherd, the world's most handsome dog. She lives in suburban Maryland and can be reached at gmarconidesign@verizon.net

www.ingramcontent.com/pod-product-compliance
Lightning Source LLC
Chambersburg PA
CBHW042313280426
43661CB00101B/1236